FOR CS, RS, KS, AND JS:
My All-Stars and the greatest home team on Earth.
Prove to the world that you can make a difference.
—RJS

FOR DAYTON AND KAI
—FC

Expand learning beyond the printed book. Download free, complementary educational resources for this book from our website, www.lerneresource.com.

Text copyright © 2013 by Robert Skead
Illustrations copyright © 2013 by Floyd Cooper

Carolrhoda Books
A division of Lerner Publishing Group, Inc.
241 First Avenue North
Minneapolis, MN 55401 U.S.A.

Website address: www.lernerbooks.com

Main body text set in ITC Cushing Std Medium 14.5/19. Typeface provided by Adobe Systems.

Library of Congress Cataloging-in-Publication Data

Skead, Robert.
    Something to prove : the great Satchel Paige vs. rookie Joe Dimaggio / by Robert Skead ; illustrated by Floyd Cooper.
       p. cm.
    ISBN: 978–0–7613–6619–5 (lib. bdg. : alk. paper)
    1. DiMaggio, Joe, 1914–1999—Juvenile literature. 2. Paige, Satchel, 1906–1982—Juvenile literature. 3. Baseball players—United States—Social conditions—Juvenile literature. 4. Discrimination in baseball—United States—History—Juvenile literature. I. Cooper, Floyd. II. Title.
    GV865.A1S5157 2013
    796.3570922—dc23 [B]   2012019709

Manufactured in the United States of America
1 – PC – 12/31/12

SOMETHING TO PROVE

THE GREAT SATCHEL PAIGE
✪ VS ✪
ROOKIE JOE DIMAGGIO

ROBERT SKEAD
✪

ILLUSTRATIONS BY
FLOYD COOPER

🍂 CAROLRHODA BOOKS ✪ *Minneapolis*

IN THE WINTER OF 1936,

New York Yankees general manager
Ed Barrow and his scout Bill Essick
needed to test a young, skinny
prospect named Joe DiMaggio.

"To see how good he is,
he has to face the best,"
said Barrow.

That's when Satchel Paige got the call. "Can you come north?" the scout asked. Satchel had been barnstorming the entire winter in Southern California. Never one to turn down an opportunity to pitch, Satchel accepted the invitation.

Satchel was the marvel of the country. He might even have been the greatest pitcher in the world. But because of the color of his skin, he was not permitted to play in the major leagues.

Word of mouth about the showdown spread. More than four thousand fans, both white and black, crammed the ballpark to watch Satchel do his magic against big leaguers.

The umpire yelled, **"PLAY BALL!"** and in the bottom of the first, Satchel dazzled the crowd with his menu of unique pitches.

Satch threw his "trouble ball," "bat dodger," and "wobbly ball," and the major leaguers went down without a hit. But things changed in the second inning when Bud Hafey and Cookie Lavagetto both whacked doubles. The major leaguers had a run on the scoreboard.

Then, in the third inning, with a runner on first and a one-run lead, it was finally Joe's turn at bat.

Joe gripped his bat and stared at the lanky right-hander who was more than sixty feet away from him. "Watch the ball," Joe said to himself.

Satchel rocked back, then forward, and then circled his throwing arm in reverse like a windmill. He reached back, kicked his left leg high in the air, and delivered his pitch. It blazed through the air and came in close to DiMaggio . . .

. . . and hit him.

Knowing Satch's masterful control, Joe was sure he had been hit on purpose. It was the pitcher's way of saying, "Don't get too cocky in the batter's box, rookie."

Joe shook it off and hustled to first base. As he took his lead, he noticed how Satchel commanded the mound. He had no doubt that Satch was the best anywhere. He was even more determined to get a hit off the star hurler.

Satch's All-Stars started the fourth inning with a walk. That runner darted to third on a single by Ebel Brooks. Next up was Ol' Satch. He glanced at his rag-tag team. He knew it was up to him to do something. He clutched his bat and strode slowly to the batter's box. (One of Satch's personal rules was to avoid running unless absolutely necessary.) The first pitch looked like a watermelon to Satch, and he drilled it for a single. The runner scored to tie the game at one run each.

For the next couple of innings, the big leaguers struggled with Satchel's strange windmill windup. They were flummoxed by his assortment of baffling pitches.

Butterflies danced in Joe's stomach as he stepped into the batter's box for the second time. He blocked out the noise of the crowd. He tried to focus on the pearly-white bullet that seemed to leave ashes in the catcher's mitt.

Satchel decided to throw the nervous rookie his "whipsey dipsey do." He started the windmill delivery, kicked his leg high, and hurled the ball. Joe watched the pitch dip and dance—and he swung and missed. He took a deep breath, readied his bat, and steadied his legs for the next serving.

"Time to cut loose my 'four-day creeper,'" thought Satch.

DiMaggio's bat collided with the ball and sent it skidding toward short. Joe jolted down the line, hoping for an infield hit, but the shortstop threw him out.

A few innings later, Joe had his next chance to prove himself—and maybe to break the tie. Keep your eyes off his windup and foot in the air. "Just watch the ball," Joe told himself.

Satchel threw Joe pitches that bent so much that they looked like a wiggle in a cyclone. Joe managed to get his bat on one of them. He sent a grounder to the second baseman for an easy out.

Satch also did everything he could to get his team on the scoreboard. He dove into first trying to beat out a hit. He slid hard into second trying to break up a double play. After the game, Satch said, "And when I wasn't batting or running, I was down at first, trying to coach those plumbers playing with me." But the Satchel Paige All-Stars still couldn't score a run.

The game went on. Joe stepped up to the plate for what could be his last at bat. "You can hit him. You know you can," he reminded himself. He stood tall in the batter's box.

On the hill, Satchel focused his eyes on the catcher's glove. "Let's see this youngster handle my midnight rider." The pitch cut through the air. Joe launched his graceful swing.

THWACK!

The ball flew off his bat and sailed over Satch's head.

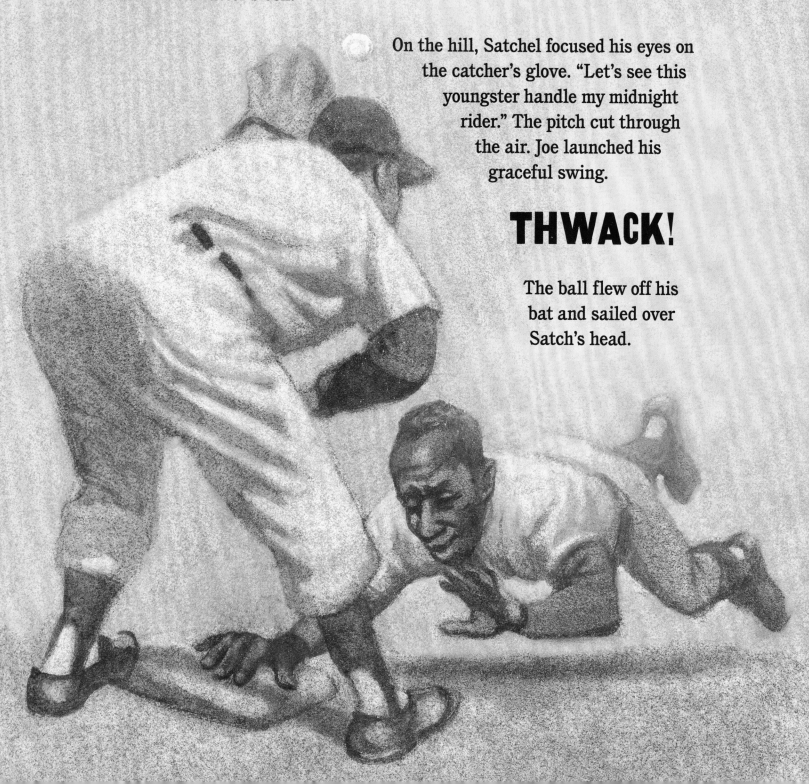

Seconds later, it landed in the center fielder's glove. Joe kicked the dirt as he stopped his sprint.

In the top of the ninth, the game was still tied. Satchel's first two hitters couldn't get on base. Then, with two outs, Ebel Brooks smashed a pitch deep into the outfield for a triple.

Now Satchel was up. Some in the crowd cheered. Others taunted him. Each fan knew that if Satch managed to get a run in, the game would be all but over. The noise from the fans was more than heard. It was felt by the players, and it went straight to their nerves. But Ol' Satch didn't fidget. He knew he had to hit the ball.

And when the pitch came in, he smacked it toward Bartell at short. He fumbled it, then fired to first. Satchel beat the throw and Brooks scored. Or so Satch thought.

"YER OUT!" yelled the first base umpire.

Satchel's eyes bulged. He knew that meant the run didn't count and the inning was over. Satch ran to the umpire and argued, but umpires never change their mind. (Years later, Satch said this ump made him so mad that his stomach got upset and he had to belch to "ease his miseries.")

No matter. Satch had a job to do. In the bottom of the ninth, he made sure the major leaguers didn't score again. He even notched two more strikeouts thanks to his trusted "trouble ball." For the entire nine innings, he had only given up three hits and he had nine strikeouts.

Still, the Satchel Paige All-Stars went down quick and easy in the top of the tenth.

The sky grew dark as Satchel took the mound in the bottom of the tenth. He got two quick outs. Then he faced the slugger Bartell, who singled for his team's first hit since the third inning.

Next at bat was Joe DiMaggio.

Satch studied DiMaggio, who had been 0 for 3 so far. Satch threw a fastball. Suddenly, Bartell took off for second. Joe watched the pitch go by for a strike, and Bartell beat the catcher's throw for a stolen base.

Satchel shook his head. He kicked the rubber with his foot. "I'm firing my bee ball," he thought.

STRIKE TWO! But the ball got past the catcher! Bartell scooted to third base.

Satch pounded the ball in his glove. This was DiMaggio's last chance to pass the test. His heart raced as he looked for Satchel's release point and the ball coming like a bullet on fire.

Satchel delivered. DiMaggio swung.

K-THUNK!

His bat skimmed the top of the ball and sent it bouncing to Satch's left. Satch lunged and his glove knocked the ball toward the second baseman. DiMaggio blazed down the first base line. But instead of charging, the second baseman froze. It seemed like an eternity passed before the sandlotter got to the ball. Finally, he scooped it up and fired to first. The ball arrived a split second after DiMaggio's foot thumped the base. Bartell scored the winning run!

Satch stood in disbelief. What more could he have done?

Bill Essick clapped from the stands.

After he composed himself, Satchel walked by the major leaguers on his way to the dugout.

DiMaggio beamed. "Now I know I can make it with the Yankees. I finally got a hit off Ol' Satch," he said.

Satch overheard Joe's comment. He and DiMaggio locked eyes. Satch could tell that he had the rookie's respect.

Immediately following the game, the Yankees scout sent a telegram to Ed Barrow with the good news.

"DIMAGGIO ALL WE HOPED HE'D BE. HIT SATCH ONE FOR FOUR."

Joe left the ballpark with his head held high. He proved he belonged in the big leagues. He joined the Yankees later that spring, and the slugger helped his team win the 1936 World Series.

Satch didn't prove he belonged in the major leagues—he'd done that years ago. Still, after hearing about Satch's performance, Phillies manager Connie Mack stated he'd pay one hundred thousand dollars to sign Satchel . . . if only he were white. Satch continued barnstorming in the off-season and played for the Pittsburgh Crawfords in the Negro Leagues that summer.

Twelve years later and one year after Jackie Robinson became the first African American major leaguer, Satchel finally got his chance. When he took the mound for the St. Louis Browns, he was the oldest rookie ever—forty-two years old! His appearance featured his array of blazing fastballs. He also hurled his "hesitation" pitch, which made one batter throw his bat forty feet up the third baseline in frustration. The Browns beat the Cleveland Indians 4–1.

AUTHOR'S NOTE

Joe DiMaggio (1914–1999) and Leroy "Satchel" Paige (1906–1982) were two of the best ballplayers of the twentieth century. You probably didn't need a book to tell you that. What I do hope this book will show you is how on one day in 1936, these two men had something to prove on a baseball diamond in California. Both men proved what they needed to prove. But what did baseball do with that proof? The answer says a lot about race and justice in America.

Here's one more pair of facts from the careers of DiMaggio and Paige. Joe DiMaggio was elected to the Baseball Hall of Fame in 1955. Satchel Paige got his plaque in Cooperstown sixteen years later—the first African American to be inducted for his accomplishments in the Negro Leagues and the third African American ballplayer overall. But even that honor was not entirely happy. Paige had to endure a public debate about whether Negro League players should be inducted into a separate wing of the hall. It was just another example of how Paige was forced to take the long way to a reward he'd obviously earned. Today, his plaque hangs in the Hall of Fame, in the main wing, where it belongs.

In the end, it might be simplest to let DiMaggio have the last word on Satch: **"THE BEST AND FASTEST PITCHER I EVER FACED."**

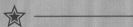

SELECTED BIBLIOGRAPHY

Paige, Leroy and David Lipman. *Maybe I'll Pitch Forever.* Lincoln: University of Nebraska Press, 1993.

Tye, Larry. *Satchel: The Life and Times of an American Legend.* New York: Random House, 2008.